For the four mermaids I know:
Mom, Michelle, Mary Sue and Karen Kelly

Mermaids

MAGIC *of the* OCEAN

Warner Treasures is a trademark of
Warner Books, Inc.

Warner Books, Inc.,
1271 Avenue of the Americas,
New York, NY 10020

 A Time Warner Company

Printed in Mexico
First Printing: March 1995
10 9 8 7 6 5 4 3 2 1

ISBN: 0-446-91010-4

Mermaids

by Barbara Jane Zitwer

MAGIC of the OCEAN

Illustrations by Robbin Gourley

WARNER ⓦ TREASURES ™

PUBLISHED BY WARNER BOOKS

A TIME WARNER COMPANY

MERMAIDS

FAR OUT AT SEA, THE WATER IS AS BLUE as the bluest cornflower and as clear as the clearest crystal, but it is very deep — deeper than any anchor cable can fathom. Many church steeples would have to be piled one on top of the other to reach from the very bottom to the surface of the water. And down in the depths live the sea folk.

— Hans Christian Andersen's
"The Little Mermaid"

From the earliest Greek tales to modern-day accounts, mermaids have appeared in literature, art and in sightings by fishermen all over the world. Long ago, mermaids, also known as morgans, were considered very dangerous. These magnificent creatures, half woman, half fish, lured sailors to their watery graves. They would sit upon rocks and torment the fishermen with their haunting voices until the men couldn't control themselves any longer and dove in after them. Mermaids are said to have lived in splendor and great riches in their castles under the sea.

Hans Christian Andersen was one of the first writers to change the image of the mermaid. His little mermaid fell in love with a sailor and gave up her voice for legs. She walked on earth and followed the sailor, but her heart was broken when he married another. She became a luminescent and wondrous spirit forever. The magic of the mermaid has lasted until today, and rather than thinking of mermaids as vile and evil, we see them as gentle, beautiful, loving creatures.

THE MERMAIDS OF IRELAND

THE IRISH THOUGHT THAT ON ST. Patrick's Day, old pagan women were turned into mermaids and thrown into the sea. In Irish, mermaids are called Murduac. In ancient Ireland, the people believed that there was a race created by the union of mortal men and mermaids. These

sons and daughters of land and sea were plagued
by sleeplessness. They were forever haunted by the
sounds of the ocean. There are Irish who believe
the descendants of such unions still exist.

Many people believed that to gaze upon a mermaid would bring you bad luck, but if the hat or
belt of one was captured, you would possess the
magical powers of the creature.

MERMAIDS ON THE BIG SCREEN

DID THERE COME A SUDDEN HORROR
upon him at last, a sudden perception of
infinite terror, and was he drawn down, swiftly and
terribly, a bubbling repentance, into those deeps?
or was she tender and wonderful to the last, and
did she wrap her arms about him and draw him
down, down until the soft waters closed above
him, down into a gentle ecstasy of death?

— H. G. Wells
    "The Sea Lady," 1902

Just as poets, writers and painters have wondered whether mermaids were wonderful or evil, so too have filmmakers.

When mermaids appeared in films, they were depicted both as wonderful, loving, magnificent creatures and as dangerous women. In the 1949 farce *Miranda* Glynnis Johns starred as the mermaid. She instantly dispelled the audience's feeling that mermaids were evil creatures. An American farce of the 1940's was called *Mr. Peabody and the Mermaid.*

However, in Truffaut's famous *Mississippi Mermaid,* Catherine Deneuve plays a mesmerizingly beautiful woman who is poisoning Jean-Paul Belmondo, the man she supposedly loves.

Daryl Hannah's best performance was as a mermaid in the hit comedy *Splash.* Her innocence and unique perspective on the hustling rat race of New York City made Tom Hanks' character fall head over heels into the sea after her, hoping to live happily every after.

Disney's animated film of *The Little Mermaid* won numerous Academy Awards and was loved by children and adults alike. In this adaptation of the Hans Christian Andersen fairy tale, Ariel, the little mermaid, loses her voice for the man she loves, gets legs to walk on earth beside him, and almost loses him. Just in the nick of time, her melodious singing is heard, and her beloved sailor falls in love with her. As opposed to the original tragic tale, the new Hollywood version has a very happy ending.

Other actresses and performers have used the image of mermaids. Madonna swam with a merman in her rock video "Cherish." Bette Midler was wheeled out onto the stage of Radio City Music Hall during one of her glitzy shows as a mermaid. Academy Award-winning actress Cher chose the unusual creature as a metaphor for the family drama *Mermaids*.

FOR DECADES, THE MERMAID PARADE has been an annual festival and parade held in Coney Island, New York, every summer. Men, women and children dress up in the most outrageous mermaid costumes and parade down the main boulevard of the once-famous seaside resort.

The Mermaid Parade occurs the first Saturday of the first day of the Summer Solstice. It celebrates Poseidon. The original idea for the parade came from the first Miss America Pageant held at the turn of the century in Atlantic City. That pageant had a parade with a mermaid theme, and the Miss America title trophy was a mermaid statuette.

The Coney Island Mermaid Parade runs in a circle along Surf Avenue to the boardwalk in Coney Island, Brooklyn. Mermaid trophies designed by local artists are given for Best

Mermaids

Mermaid Costume, Best Home Float, Best Marching Group, Best Poseidon Costume. Every year there is a celebrity Queen Mermaid and King Poseidon. Stars of TV and stage who have been Queen Mermaids at the parade are Duff from MTV, Daisey Egan from the Tony-winning play *The Secret Garden,* and Joe Franklin!

According to the organizer of the parade, a fifty-year-old woman has three years in a row won for best mermaid costume. Two of the more outrageous mermaids were one whose tail was made entirely of paper plates, the other of rubber gloves! The Mermaid Parade at Coney Island is a real "anything goes" fun family outing, where creativity and home crafts and design rule the day.

THE MIRACLE OF THE MERMAID BALLOON
(based on a true story)

ONCE UPON A TIME THERE WAS A LITTLE girl who lived in Oregon state on the farthest shore. Her father was tragically killed in a car accident. The little girl loved her father so much and couldn't come to terms with his untimely death. She was inconsolable and would visit his grave and cry and cry. She stopped talking and not her mother, nor her friends, nor her relatives could get the little girl to speak or smile.

One day the girl's mother brought home the video of *The Little Mermaid.* In some way, the story of Ariel touched the child so that she ran out and asked her mother to buy her an Ariel balloon. Attached to the balloon was a letter that she had written to her father in heaven. She went to his gravesite and let the balloon fly way up into the sky.

The mermaid balloon took flight . . . all the way to a little town called Mermaid in eastern Canada. It landed in the back-yard of a family who immediately read the touching letter the little girl had written to her father in heaven.

The father living in Mermaid decided to write back to the girl and sent her a book about how a mermaid took a sick child up to heaven, which was filled with bright light and love, and the mermaid kept the child company.

The child in Oregon couldn't believe her eyes when she received the package in the mail from Mermaid. After reading the spiritual story about the mermaid and the hereafter, only then did she come to terms with her father's death, believing that he was being watched over by the kindly and angelic mermaid.

It was a miraculous occurrence to all involved that the mermaid balloon found its way over an entire country to a town called Mermaid . . . and then returned to its sender to bring her love and peace.

A CITY BENEATH THE SEA

IN A VILLAGE NOT FAR FROM LUCERNE IN Switzerland a fable is told that concerns a mermaid. The Swiss called a mermaid a "nix." The nixes would leave their watery home in the Lake of Zug and wander around the village at night. The only way you could tell a nix from a mortal girl was by the water that dripped from the hem of her skirt.

One night a nix fell in love with a tall and handsome farmer from the village, and he fell in love with her. She charmed him into returning to her home in the lake and by using her magical powers was able to allow him to breathe the water, like a fish. They lived happily for a while, but it wasn't long before the man became despondent and missed his family and friends. He was becoming more and more unhappy as the days went on.

Rather than returning the man to the land, the nix, who was full of love for this man, brought the entire village under the sea to him! It is said that when you peer into the Lake of Zug, you can sometimes, on a moonlit night, see all the villagers moving about and living happily under the sea.

MERMAIDS USE THIS SPECIAL OINT-ment to turn into mortals, and to keep looking young forever. They rub the ointment onto their eyes and are transformed into women, free to roam the villages or towns, have fun, dance and be merry. They have no inhibitions and are full of self-confidence. There is a lot of conjecture on what is contained in their little mother-of-pearl vials. This is the first time ever that the secret of mermaid essence has become available to you, gentle readers. And it is a recipe you can make for yourselves. Try it: Mermaid essence is sure to work wonders.

Go to the sea and gather a pound of fresh seaweed. Keep the seaweed in a large bucket of seawater. Let the seaweed set in the seawater for several hours before you start the natural prepa-ration. Drain all the water out and blend the sea-weed in a food processor or blender, or use a

large, sharp cutting knife to chop the seaweed into fine bits.

Take three small bowls. In one bowl pour half a cup of fresh coconut milk. You can purchase coconuts in almost every grocery store. Refrigerate for twenty minutes.

Crack three eggs and separate the whites from the yolks. Put the whites into the second bowl and set the yokes aside. You will only be using the whites for the ointment.

Squeeze the juice of three large cucumbers into the third bowl.

After twenty minutes, take the three mixtures and fold them one at a time into the large bowl filled with the seaweed. After all the ingredients are smoothly combined, apply the mask to your face. Lie back in a soothing bathtub filled with Dead Sea salt and relax. Think back to the sea, to all the times you frolicked in the ocean, and imagine you are a wondrous, unique creature — a mermaid! After half an hour, rub the mask

off your face. Your pores will be stimulated;
you'll feel relaxed and younger. You'll have the
"essence of mermaid."

MERMAID BEAUTY SECRETS

MERMAIDS ALWAYS HAVE LONG
flowing hair and keep it that way by sitting
upon a rock brushing thousands of strokes. When
they look in their mirrors after hours of brushing,
the mermaids see their glowing locks glisten in the
bright light of the day, and they are finished. One
basic key to mermaid beauty is to "know thy
face"!

Favorite attire is a cap,
most often red, a cloak
or shawl, and of

course they always carry their
hairbrush, mirrors and capes. A mermaid's gar-

ments have great power. A man or woman who steals a garment from a mermaid has unbelievable luck. Their dreams come true, but they must hold hostage the poor creature who forever searches for her belongings. Once she recovers them, she disappears, taking all her good luck with her.

So powerful is the myth of a mermaid's garments that when a child is born

with a caul or veil over its face, it is believed that such a child is blessed and will never drown.

LOVE RULES TO FOLLOW IF YOU ARE DATING A MERMAID

1. Never betray her; the wrath of a mermaid is unfathomable and endless. As beautiful and sweet as her nature can be, so it can be as vindictive and evil. Above all, mermaids value faithfulness.

2. Never eat any food served by a mermaid in her underwater cave; you will never be able to return to land, should you want to.

3. Never peer at her through a keyhole in the bathroom on a Saturday — it's her day to relax in the tub, and her tail comes out in full bloom.

4. Buy her a new gold or mother-of-pearl mirror for her birthday.

5. A new and strong hairbrush is sure to make her happy.

6. Play gospel and other church music — it's music to her ears.

7. Mermaids love to collect seashells — if you give her a beautiful shell, she might grant you a

miraculous wish.

8. Mermaids love to be kissed; they are very romantic.

9. Prepare a wonderful meal of oysters on the half-shell, raw lobsters and clams. One way to a mermaid's heart is through her stomach.

10. Rub hot coconut oil over her tail — it smoothes her scales and will drive her wild with desire!

Rules

MERMAID BABY NAMES

THESE ARE NAMES THAT HAVE BEEN given to mermaids throughout the centuries. They would suit any darling little mermaid baby of yours!

The Caribbean: (ancient names for mermaids)
Mama Alo
Mamo Jo

Hollywood: (star of Disney's *The Little Mermaid*)
Ariel

Greece: (ancient Greek name for mermaids)
Artemis

Celtic lands: (Celtic name for mermaids)
Marie Morgane

Babylonia: (names of Babylonian mermaid goddesses)
Melusina
Lilith

France:
Undine (name of Fouqué's mermaid in *Undine*)
Melusina: from French medieval legend and found in Jean d'Arra's *Chronicle,* 1387

Holland: (name of Dutch mermaid in the story "The Lost Sea" by Jan de Hartog)
Mensje

Java: (ancient names of Javanese mermaid goddesses)
Loro Kidul
Batu Loro Kidul

England:
Miranda, star of the
British film *Miranda*

Sabrina: immortalized by
poet John Milton, she was the ill-
fated sea nymph of a tale from the
ancient Midlands.

Russia:
Rusalka, in the Dvorák
opera *The Mermaid*

Ghana: (goddess of the
sea rock in Ghana)
Tahbi-yin

Early Christian name:
Nereides, from Pliny's
Natural History

Early Welsh name:

Branwen, meaning "white bosom"

Early Irish names:

Liban: from a myth of a young girl drowned in the Lake of Copse, now known as Lough Neagh. She was swept away in a flood and saved in an underwater cavern with her pet dog. After a year, she was unhappy and asked to be turned into a salmon. She was turned into a mermaid, and her dog became an otter.

Mergelt

Mermaids

Icelandic:
Margyr: people in Greenland in the twelfth century referred to mermaids with this name.

Norwegian:
Havfrus

Finland:
Aino: the mermaid heroine of a Finnish tale told since the 1500s.

Lapland:
Akkriva: Lap mermaid goddess

German:
Meerfrau
Nixe: name for mermaid in German folktales
Merriminni: from Jakob Grimm's *Teutonic Mythology*, 1825
Lorelei: from High German, *lur* (to lurk) and *lai* (rock)—describes a mermaid's habit of lurking on the rocks.

Japan:
Mu Jima
Ningyo

Peru:
Tempuleague

Guiana:
Orehu

Hawaii:
Hawaiian tales describe mermaids as shark-goddesses in their fables. These are the names of heroines of some fables:

Ko-le-a
Kaala
Kuahupah

SO, IF MERMAIDS DON'T EXIST, WHAT ARE THEY?

THERE ARE MANY EXPLANATIONS FOR all the mermaids seen over the centuries.

One explanation is that a mermaid is really a seal. Seals have very cute and humanlike faces, and they nurse their offspring, which may give females the appearance of having breasts. If a sailor had too much to drink, he might mistake a cute little seal for the mermaid of his dreams. Seals also like to lounge on rocks, as mermaids are said to do. Seals like to make musical-sounding noises, and mermaids love to sing.

Another theory is that the great mana- tees of the ocean, which also nurse their young, have been mistaken for mermaids. As manatees are quite rare and not often seen, their appearance, especially from a distance, could be construed as that of a mer- maid.

Some say that mermaids simply do not exist at all; but famous historical figures like Henry Hudson and many religious figures have vouched for their existence and have given detailed reports of their sightings. The existence of mermaids might be compared to that of aliens from other planets here on earth. Some people disregard the possibility totally; whereas people from Harvard professors to policemen have sworn under oath that they have encountered other beings, even passing lie detector tests.

Then there are those who say that mermaids are walruses. This is the most outrageous attempt to explain mermaids — mermen, maybe. Mermen are not known for their beauty, so a walrus could be mistaken for one despite its bulk, whiskers and beard, teeth, short neck, double chin and heavy brows. It's no wonder that mermaids prefer mortal men to their kind. Wouldn't you?

WHAT DOES A MERMAID WANT?

LIVING UNDERNEATH THE SEA IN A
castle of richness and glamor seems mighty
enticing. Why have mermaids pervaded our minds
and hearts for centuries, why do they appear to
humans, and what is it that they want?

Mermaids are a little like the Tin Man, the
Scarecrow, the Cowardly Lion and Dorothy from
The Wizard of Oz. They are searching for human
qualities and want to interact with mortals.

Mermaids want souls.

Mermaids want love.

Mermaids want to help mortals, grant wishes
and bring great happiness — it is in their nature
to do so.

Mermaids want to sing to a man's ear.

But like the Wicked Witch of the East, a
Mermaid's wrath is unmatched if she is taken
advantage of — yet she ventures to the mortal
world, knowing she might be captured and

enslaved until she finds a release. Mermaids are adventurers and explorers.

THE MERMAID CLUB

At Bread Street's Mermaid having dined and
   merry
Proposed to go to Holborn in a wherry.
                   — Beaumont

    Sir Walter Raleigh made this tavern famous in 1603 in England by turning it into a literary hangout. Writers and artists would eat, drink, be merry and talk literature at the Mermaid. If you stepped back in time, you might on any night come across men such as Shakespeare, Beaumont, Fletcher and Raleigh sitting at long wooden tables enjoying themselves. Ben Jonson frequented the place. A privileged person reveals in an old diary from that period one of the riotous exchanges between Shakespeare and Jonson:

Mermaids

Many were the wit combats betwix Shakespeare and Ben Jonson, which two I beheld like a Spanish galleon and an English man-O-war; Master Jonson, like the former, as built the English man-of-war, lesser in bulk, but lighter in sailing, could turn with all tides, tack about, and take advantage of all winds, by the quickness of his wit and invention.

Christopher Marlowe also frequented the Mermaid with his pals Shakespeare and Jonson, and in his poem "Hero and Leander," he mentions mermaids:

Leander strived; the waves about him wound,
And pulled him to the bottom, where the
    ground
Was strewn with pearl, and in low coral groves
Sweet singing mermaids sported with their
    loves
On heaps of heavy gold, and took great
    pleasure
To spurn in careless sort the shipwreck
    treasure.

The Mermaid Tavern has disappeared, but in
1955, the Mermaid Theatre opened on the old
site of the famous literary bar. Jon Taylor, a seven-
teenth-century poet who called himself the "Water
Poet of England," declared that there were at least
ten Mermaid Taverns in London.

Sabrina fair,
    Listen where thou art sitting
Under the glassie, cool, transluscent wave,
    In twisted braids of Lillies knitting
The loose train of thy amber-dropping hair,
    Listen for honour's sake,
Goddess of the silver lake,
    Listen and save!

                 * * *

Wherewith she sits on golden rocks
Sleeking her soft alluring locks . . .
             — Milton, "Masque of Comus"

White limbs, unrobed in a crystal air,
Sweet faces, rounded arms, and bosoms prest
Two little harps of gold. . .
                 — Tennyson, "Sea Fairies"

Mermaids

From *The Book of Marvels of India* written over a thousand years ago by Buzurg ibn Shahriyar of Hurmuz:

> The sailors, by signs, asked if any other wares were for sale, and in response the natives confronted us with the most beautiful slaves we had ever seen, and the merriest, dancing, playing, frolicking and fooling between themselves. Their bodies were plump and soft to touch as cream. So light they were and so lively that every moment, you thought, they were ready to take wing. Only their heads were tiny, and below their flanks, they had a kind of wing or fluke like turtles.
>
> When the voyage ended, an old man told

the crew that the islands where chance had led
them were known as the
Islands of Fish, from
which he originally
came. He explained
the amphibious
nature of the slaves by
saying that men former-
ly coupled with the
females of the sea-
creatures, and the
women gave them-
selves to the males

of the same kind. From these unions were born a race of beings who shared the nature of both mother and father, and presently bred among themselves. Long has it been so. And we are equally the natives of the sea and land, dividing our ancestry between men and fish.

From Shakespeare's *A Midsummer Night's Dream*:

Though rememb'rest
Since once I sat upon a promontory,
And heard a mermaid on a dolphin's back
Uttering such dulct and harmonious breath,
That the rude sea grew civil at her song,
And certain stars shot madly from their
     spheres
To hear the sea-maid's music.

From explorer Henry Hudson's log, two months after he sailed from St. Katherine's Dock on his second attempt to find "the passage," June 15, 1608:

This morning, one of our companie looking overboard saw a Mermaid, and calling up some of the companie to see her, one more came up, and by that time shee was come close to the ship's side, looking earnestly on the men: a little after, a Sea came and overturned her: From the Navill upward her backe and breasts were like a womans (as they say that saw her) her body as big as one of us; her skin very white; and long haire hanging down behinde, of color blacke; in her going down they saw her tayle, which was like the tayle of a Porposees, and speckled like a Macrell. Their names that saw her were Thomas Hiller and Robert Raynar.

45

From *Undine,* by Friedrich de la Motte
Fouqué:

Undine is one of the most romantic fables
about mermaids. Once upon a time in a forest an old couple had a beautiful baby daughter. The husband was a fisherman and one
day there was a huge flood and their child
disappeared, thought to be dead. The poor
parents grieved so for their daughter, but
miraculously one day in that same forest
they found a tiny infant girl, Undine.
Undine was actually a mermaid at heart.

Undine grew and lived a happy life. Mean-
while the original daughter of the fisherman
and his wife had been adopted by a royal couple and became engaged to a Prince. She
sent the Prince to the forest on an errand of
derring-do and it was there that he laid his
eyes on the beautiful Undine and instantly

fell in love and married her. Theirs was not meant to be a happy marriage because although they loved each other, the Prince felt she was otherworldly and she was never quite accepted by his court.

The god of the sea wanted Undine back and she warned her husband never to curse her, while they were on the sea. While in a storm, he forgot his promise, cursed her and she disappeared forever under the waves. The Prince returned to his kingdom a broken man and died soon after. At his funeral, the long lost Undine appeared as a white apparition and turned herself into a fountain.

From the Arabian *1,001 Nights*:

Hasan of Bassorah discovered ten swan-maidens in a garden whose door he was forbidden to unlock, but into which he penetrated. At the sight of him, the maidens doffed their plumage and plunged into the pool. Hasan fell in love with their queen, "his heart taken in the net of her love."

From Euripides, *The Trojan Women* (480 B.C.):

Up from the Aegean caverns, pool by pool
Of blue salt sea, where feet most beautiful
Of Nereid maidens weave beneath the foam
Their long sea-dances, I, their lord, am come,
Poseidon of the Sea.

L ITERATURE, ART, RELIGION AND FILM have depicted the existence and sighting of mermaids since humankind's earliest time. Do they exist? Some think yes, others think no.

Mermaids can exist in many ways and many forms. There are women with dimples, supposedly left over from their lives as fish.

The beautiful Irish red-headed women are perhaps descendants of their Irish mermaid sisters, who wore red caps.

Some humans still have traces of ancestral fish gills that must be surgically removed. Were these gills from their former times as mermaids?

There are those women who love to swim and are fearless in the ocean; they are said to swim like mermaids.

And some think mermaids are the romantic longings of sailors. But what is love and who is who? Love is in the eyes of the beholder and maybe, just maybe, mermaids do exist for many of us. For me, they do.

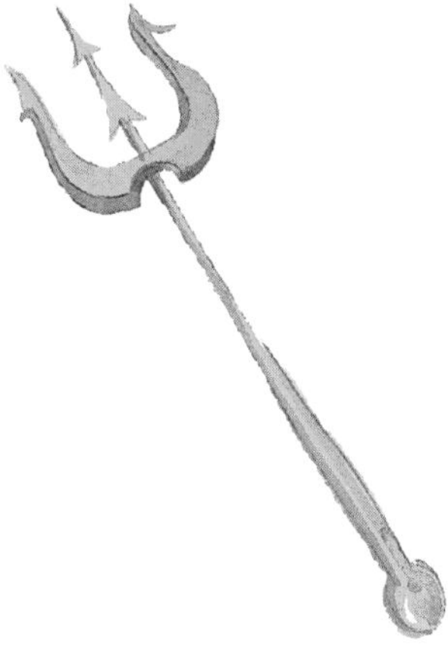

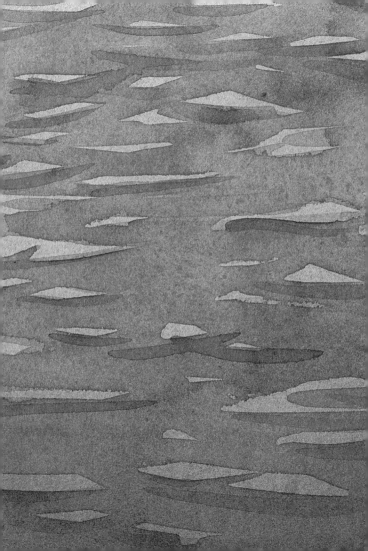